# I SPY
## ADVENTURE
### 4 PICTURE RIDDLE BOOKS

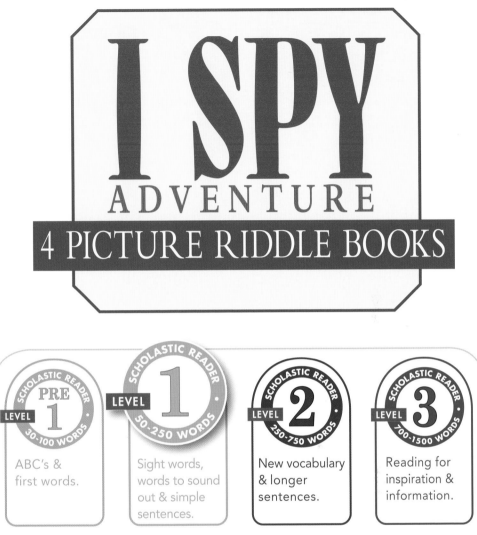

**SCHOLASTIC READER**
**PRE LEVEL 1**
**30-100 WORDS**
ABC's & first words.

**SCHOLASTIC READER**
**LEVEL 1**
**50-250 WORDS**
Sight words, words to sound out & simple sentences.

**SCHOLASTIC READER**
**LEVEL 2**
**250-750 WORDS**
New vocabulary & longer sentences.

**SCHOLASTIC READER**
**LEVEL 3**
**700-1500 WORDS**
Reading for inspiration & information.

Based on the best research about how children learn to read, Scholastic Readers are developed under the supervision of reading experts and are educator approved.

| BEGINNING TO DEVELOPING READER | GRADE LEVEL | GUIDED READING LEVEL | LEXILE® LEVEL | WORD COUNT |
|---|---|---|---|---|
| Level 1 | Pre-K–1 | G | NP | 160-174 |

"Scholastic Readers are designed to support your child's efforts to learn how to read at every age and every stage. Enjoy helping your child learn to read and love to read."

Francie Alexander
CHIEF ACADEMIC OFFICER
SCHOLASTIC INC.

*I Spy a Butterfly*
*I Spy a Balloon*
*I Spy Lightning in the Sky*
*I Spy an Apple*

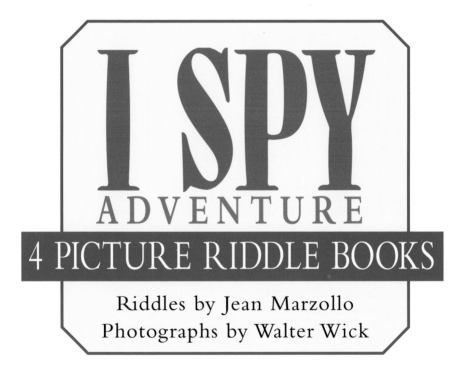

# I SPY
## ADVENTURE
### 4 PICTURE RIDDLE BOOKS

Riddles by Jean Marzollo
Photographs by Walter Wick

Cartwheel Books / New York
An imprint of Scholastic Inc.

*I Spy a Butterfly* (978-0-439-73865-1); Text copyright © 2006 by Jean Marzollo. "Chain Reaction" from *I Spy Mystery* © 1993 by Walter Wick; "Flight of Fancy," "Blast Off," "Sweet Dreams," and "Ballerina" from *I Spy Fantasy* © 1994 by Walter Wick; "Be My Valentine" and "Sorting and Classifying" from *I Spy School Days* © 1995 by Walter Wick; "Full Moon at Dawn," "Good Morning," and "The Empty Hall" from *I Spy Spooky Night* © 1996 by Walter Wick.

*I Spy a Balloon* (978-0-439-73864-4); Text copyright © 2006 by Jean Marzollo. "Toys in the Attic," "Make Believe," and "Silhouettes" from *I Spy* © 1992 by Walter Wick; "Creepy Crawly Cave" from *I Spy Fun House* © 1993 by Walter Wick; "The Secret Note" and "The Ghost in the Attic" from *I Spy Mystery* © 1993 by Walter Wick; "Old-fashioned School," "Levers, Ramps, and Pulleys," and "Mapping" from *I Spy School Days* © 1995 by Walter Wick; "A Blazing Fire" from *I Spy Spooky Night* © 1996 by Walter Wick.

*I Spy Lightning in the Sky* (978-0-439-68052-3); Text copyright © 2005 by Jean Marzollo. Illustrations copyright © 1999 by Walter Wick. All images by Walter Wick taken from *I Spy Treasure Hunt*. Published by Scholastic Inc. in 1999.

*I Spy an Apple* (978-0-545-22095-8); Text copyright © 2011 by Jean Marzollo. "Nutcracker Sweets" from *I Spy Christmas* © 1992 by Walter Wick; "1, 2, 3..." from *I Spy School Days* © 1995 by Walter Wick; "View from Duck Pond Inn" from *I Spy Treasure Hunt* © 1999 by Walter Wick; "A Is for..." from *I Spy School Days* © 1995 by Walter Wick; "Storybook Theater" from *I Spy School Days* © 1995 by Walter Wick; "Masquerade" from *I Spy Mystery* © 1993 by Walter Wick; "Sand Castle" from *I Spy Fantasy* © 1994 by Walter Wick; "Blast Off!" from *I Spy Fantasy* © 1994 by Walter Wick; "1, 2, 3..." from *I Spy School Days* © 1995 by Walter Wick; "Treasure at Last!" from *I Spy Treasure Hunt* © 1999 by Walter Wick.

ISBN 978-1-4351-3984-8

12  11  10  9  8  7  6  5  4                    15  16  17  18  19/0

Printed in China  38 • This printing, November 2015.

This custom edition is published exclusively for Sandy Creek by Scholastic Inc.

*For Andrew, Bryan,*
*and Matthew McNamara,*
*with thanks to Dave*
*—J.M.*

*To Abigail Dodge*
*—W.W.*

# I SPY

## A BUTTERFLY

Riddles by Jean Marzollo
Photographs by Walter Wick

I spy

a butterfly,

 a silver jack,

a fish,

 a mask,

and a yellow tack.

I spy

a deer,

 a little blue sail,

a window frog,

and an elephant's tail.

I spy

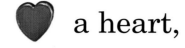 a heart,

a lightbulb,

 a spoon,

and two men ready

for a trip to the moon.

I spy

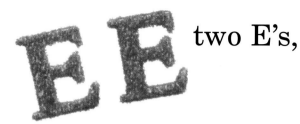 two E's,

a red-and-yellow star,

 a hot dog,

a lion,

 and a star on a car.

I spy

a yo-yo,

 a crayon,

a duck,

 a blue kangaroo,

and a small cement truck.

I spy

a paper clip,

 a plaid bow tie,

two fans,

a cage,

 and a butterfly.

FROM
NUTCRACKER
SUITE

I spy

sunglasses,

a wooden guitar,

a deer,

three crayons,

and a little red car.

I spy

a ghost,

a fork,

a bat,

and a dark green face

with a bright yellow hat.

I spy

a carriage,

 a sea horse,

a clock,

 two frying pans,

a snake,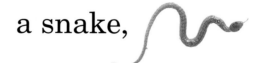

 and a lock.

I spy

a spoon,

a clear glass whale,

a pair of pliers,

and a shadow cat's tail.

# I spy two matching words.

elephant's tail

shadow cat's tail

clock

# I spy two matching words.

bright yellow hat

heart

red-and-yellow star

# I spy two words that start with the letter F.

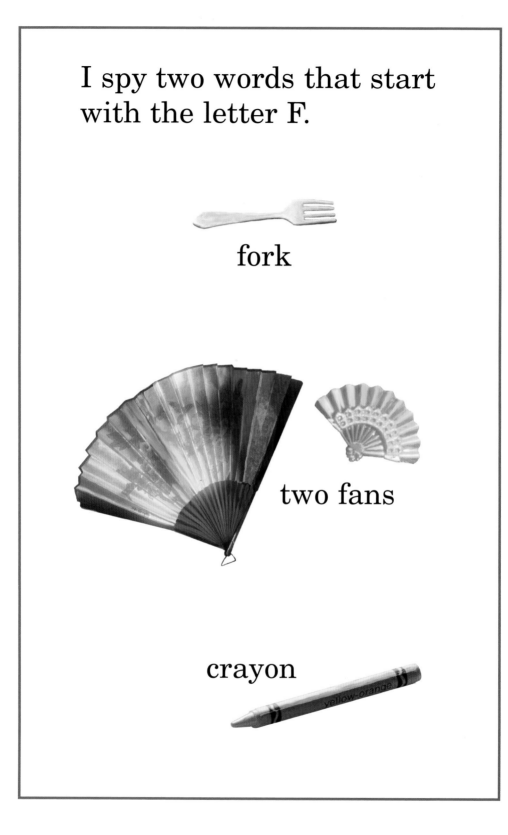

fork

two fans

crayon

I spy two words that start with the letter W.

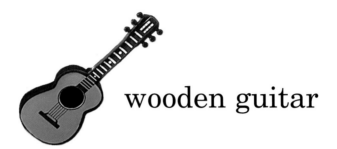
wooden guitar

mask

clear glass whale

I spy two words that end with the letter G.

hot dog

lion

window frog

I spy two words that end with the letter E.

snake

cage

bat

# I spy two words that rhyme.

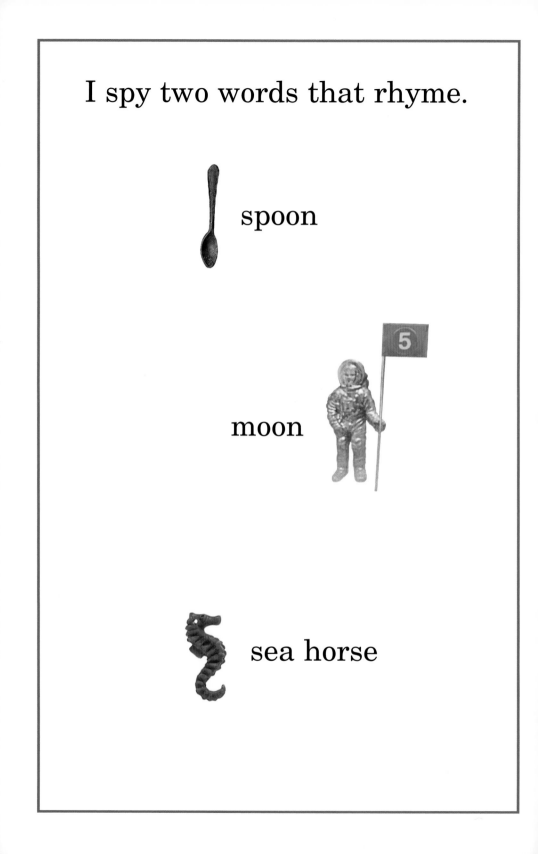

spoon

moon

sea horse

# I spy two words that rhyme.

bow tie

kangaroo

butterfly

*For Uncle Chris,
with thanks to Dave
—J.M.*

*To Edward Helt
—W.W.*

# I SPY
## A BALLOON

Riddles by Jean Marzollo
Photographs by Walter Wick

I spy

an egg,

 a marble,

a three,

 a clown's white hat,

and a block with a G.

I spy

a ship,

 a multicolored ball,

a cat,

old string,

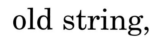

and A PARASOL.

Georgie Porgie, pudding and pie,
Kissed the girls and made them cry,
When the boys came out to play
Georgie Porgie ran away.

S

CAMEL

A PARASOL

A PUMPKIN

$2.50

MmNn

A POUND OF BUTTER

30 CENTS

BUTTER

35 CENTS

PROBL

CLASSES

OLS.

22

with we" so they came and had
Somesucking Pig for Break
Fast M$ Rogs asked if he and
M$L could go out with them
Oh yes, ofcorse you can it we wil
forhey all started of anyou some
Then suddenly M$B bumped up
with a scream and declared
he was dead! You donkey
said M$R. With this M$ London

I spy

a skateboard,

 a letter-block L,

SCIENCE,

 a fork,

a balloon,

and a bell.

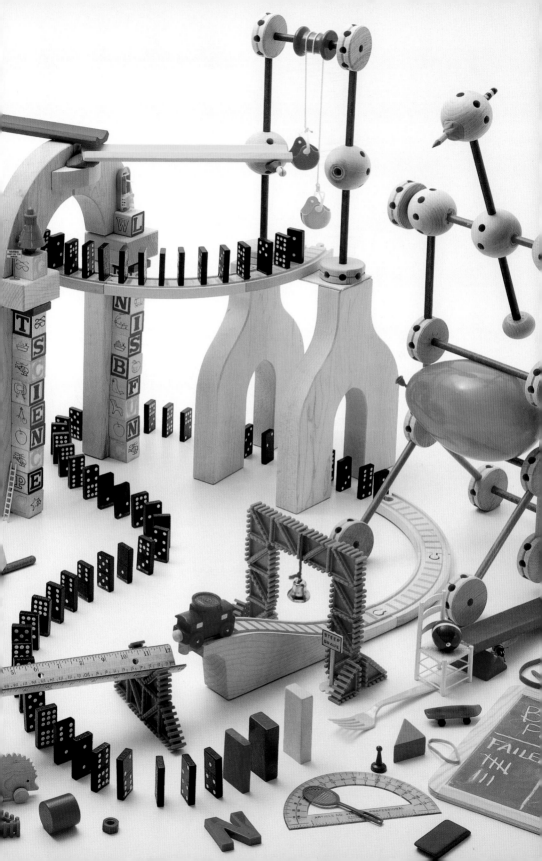

I spy  a deer,

a lonely shoe,

 a giraffe,

a rat,

 and a skeleton, too.

I spy

an elephant,

 a clown's white face,

a rubber band,

and a dress made of lace.

I spy

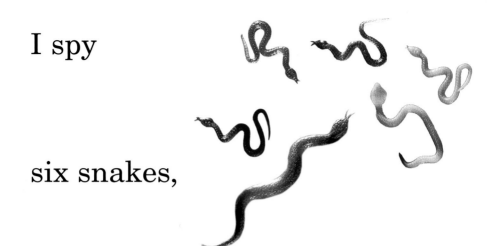

six snakes,

a scorpion's tail,

a lizard's tongue,

and the shell of a snail.

I spy

a plane,

a shovel,

three springs,

a lock,

a crab,

and a baby with wings.

I spy

a brush,

a lady on toes,

a spider,

a ball,

and a bunny in clothes.

I spy

a bench,

 a red fire truck,

a painter,

 a bus,

25,

 and a duck.

I spy  a bottle,

a man with a hat,

a 2 on a block,

and a tiny black cat.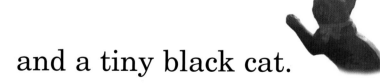

# I spy two matching words.

white hat

white face

bottle

# I spy two matching words.

cat

bus

a tiny black cat

# I spy two words that start with the letters SK.

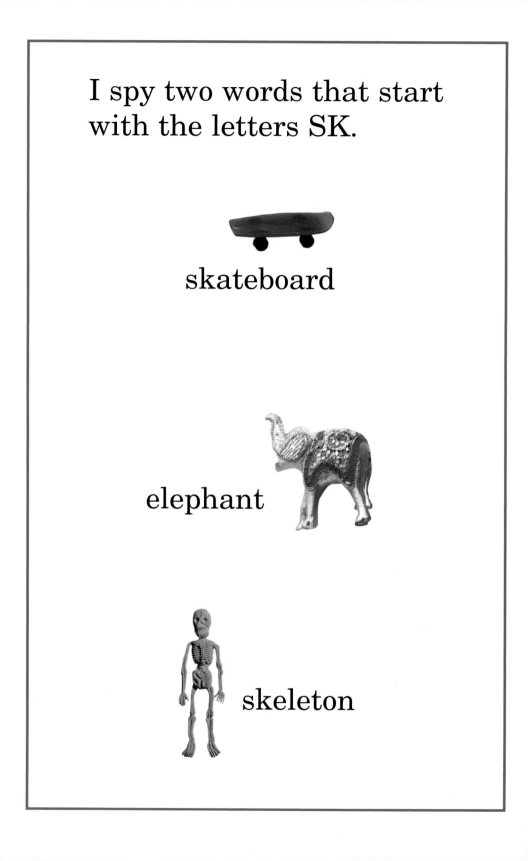

skateboard

elephant

skeleton

I spy two words that start with the letters SH.

shovel

shoe

giraffe

# I spy two words that end with the letters CK.

lock

brush

block

I spy two words that end with an apostrophe plus s ('s).

scorpion's tail

rubber band

lizard's tongue

# I spy two words that rhyme.

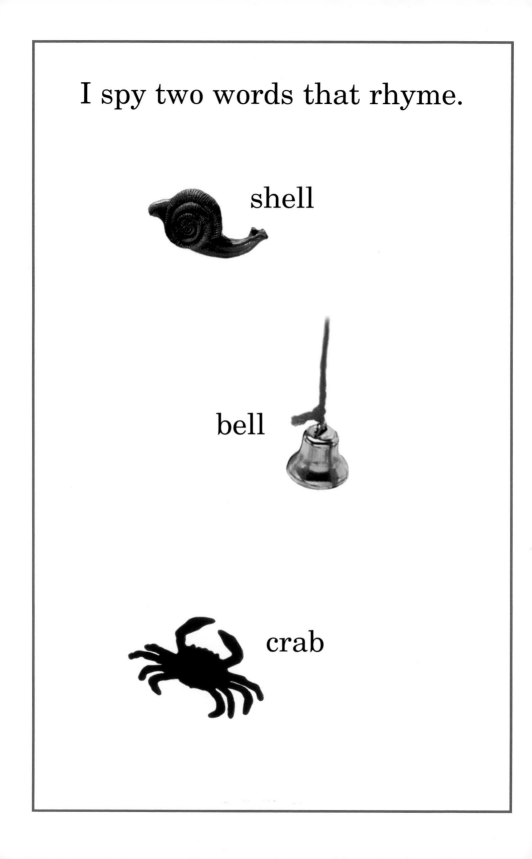

shell

bell

crab

# I spy two words that rhyme.

egg

rat

hat

*For Allen
and his cousin Dave
—J.M.*

*For Maya Griffin
—W.W.*

# I SPY

## LIGHTNING IN THE SKY

Riddles by Jean Marzollo
Photographs by Walter Wick

I spy

a truck,

a lighthouse light,

 a jack,

and a lightning bolt
at night.

I spy

a tiny toy cannon,

 a 3,

a brown starfish,

 and two shells from the sea.

I spy

a stop sign,

a wet blue duck,

Sharky's shack,

 and a yellow truck.

I spy

a shell,

two oars,

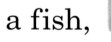 LOST CAT,

a fish,

and a biker in a red hat.

I spy

a screw,

 a pair of wings,

a key in a jar,

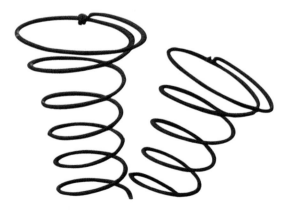

and two large springs.

I spy

a ladder,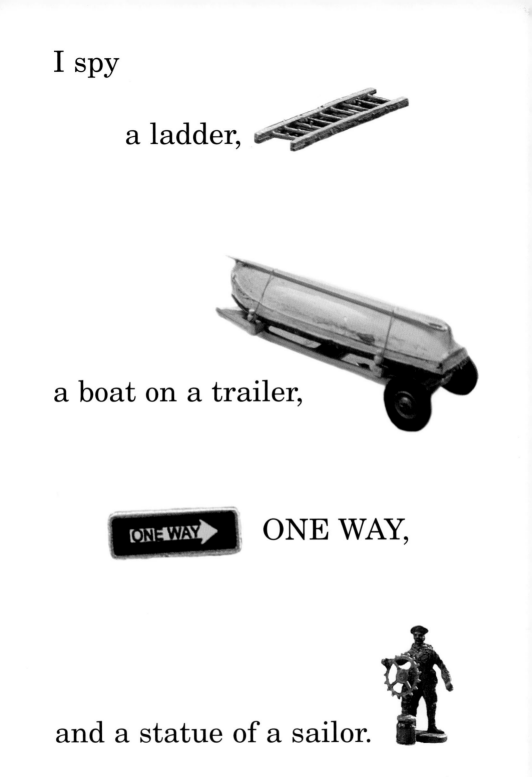

a boat on a trailer,

ONE WAY,

and a statue of a sailor.

I spy

a starfish,

a seagull,

a seal,

a magnifying glass,

and a silver
ship's wheel.

I spy

an arrow,

a pail on a string,

a furry groundhog,

and a tire swing.

I spy

an oar,

a ship,

a plane,

TOW-AWAY ZONE,

and a rusty chain.

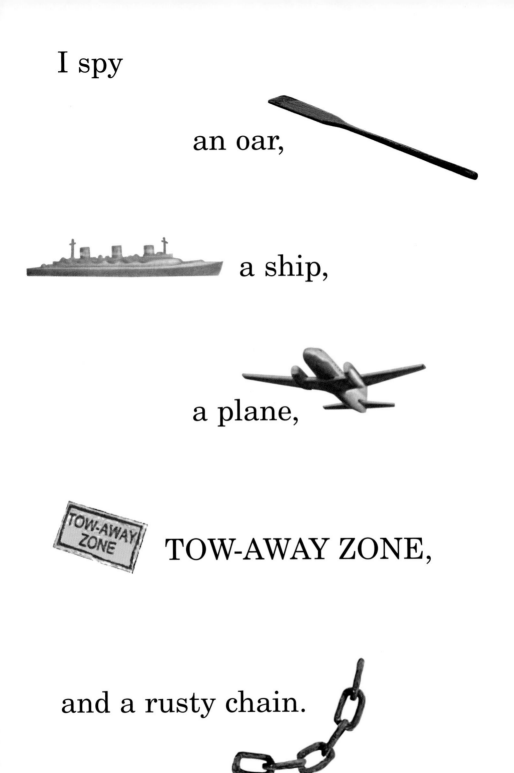

I spy

 a trash can,

a red suitcase,

 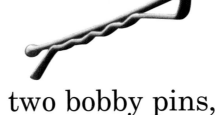 two bobby pins,

and a president's face.

I spy two matching words.

tiny toy cannon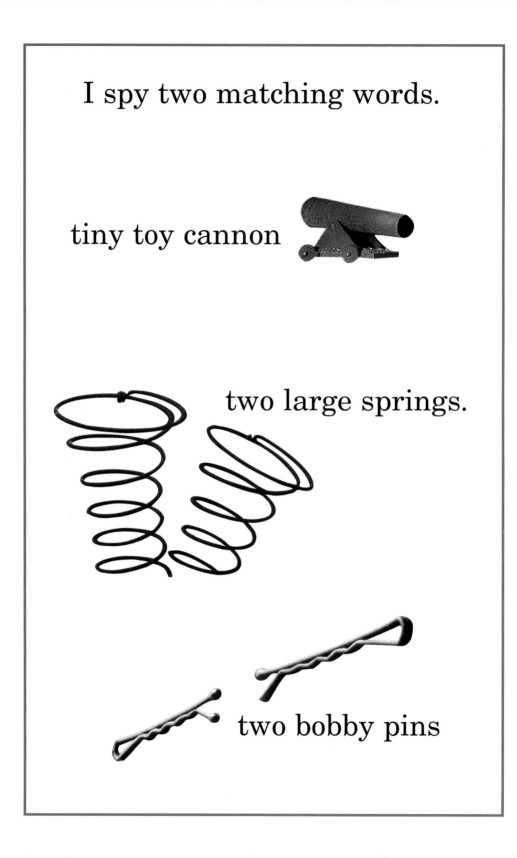

two large springs.

two bobby pins

# I spy two matching words.

statue of a sailor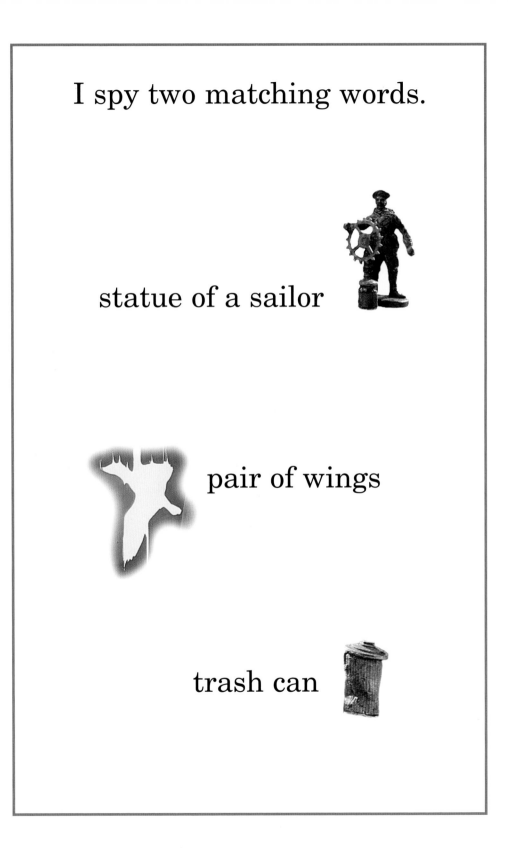

pair of wings

trash can

# I spy two words that start with the letter S.

 seal

suitcase

 groundhog

I spy two words that start with the letter L.

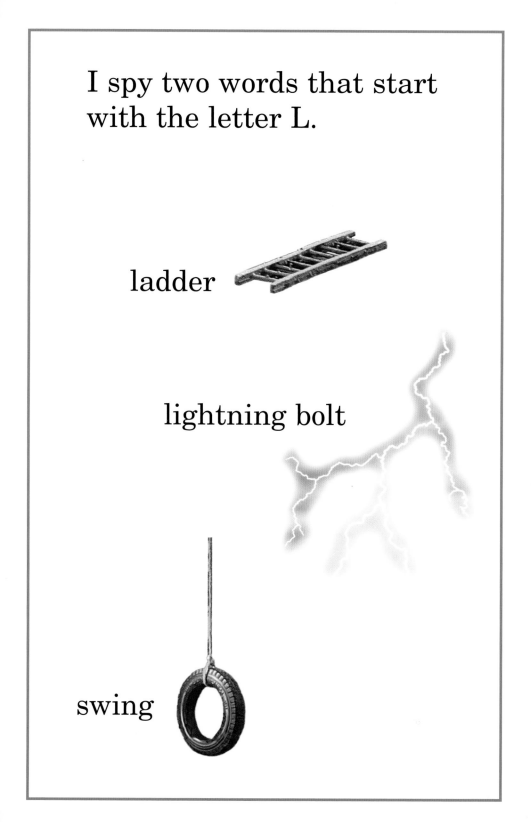

ladder

lightning bolt

swing

I spy two words that end with the letters LL.

seagull

shell

wheel

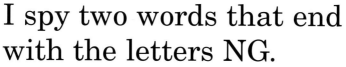

I spy two words that end with the letters NG.

pail on a string

tire swing

statue

# I spy two words that rhyme.

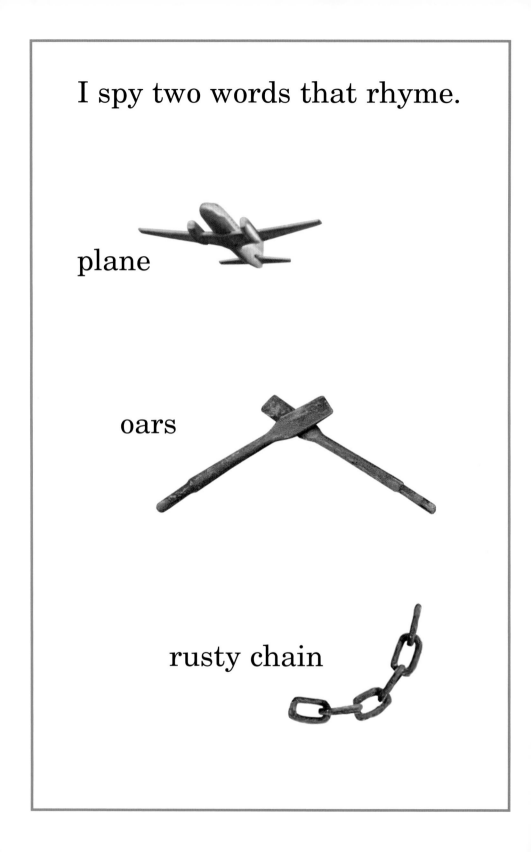

plane

oars

rusty chain

# I spy two words that rhyme.

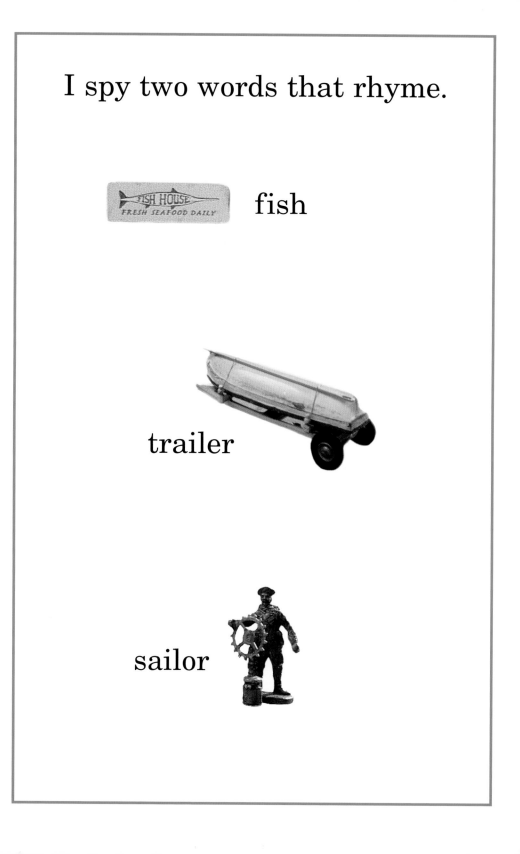

fish

trailer

sailor

*For Benjamin Miles Nieves*
*—J.M.*

*For Corey and Liliana Perriello*
*—W.W.*

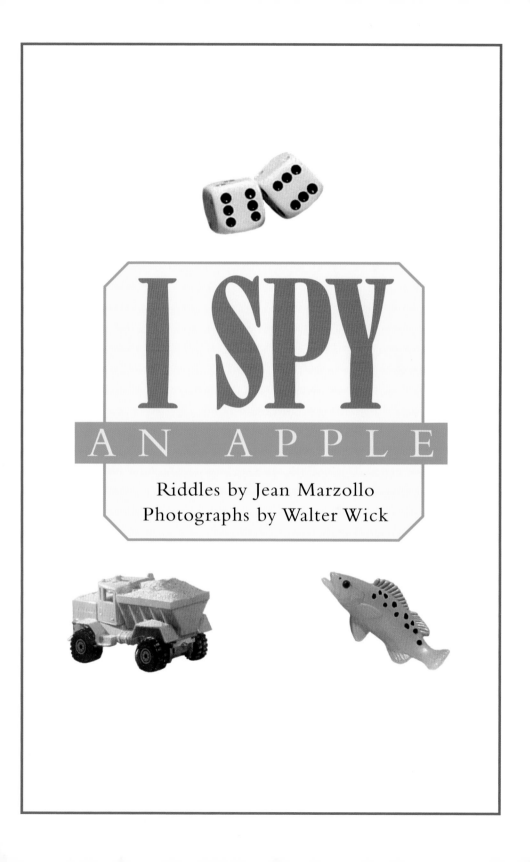

# I SPY
## AN APPLE

Riddles by Jean Marzollo
Photographs by Walter Wick

I spy

an apple,

 an orange, too,

a yellow gumdrop,

and a ribbon of blue.

I spy

a tomato,

 a yellow shoe,

a silly clown,

 and a bug that's blue.

I spy

 a yellow car,

and MAPS,

 an ice cream cone,

and two red caps.

I spy

 a bunch of bananas,

a Z,

 a little hot dog,

a horse,

 and a 3.

I spy

four yellow stars,

   a crown,

a skunk,

   a spoon,

and a bunny that's brown.

I spy

a bird,

 a mask that's blue,

a jar of glitter,

 and the number 32.

I spy

a sailboat,

 a surfboard that's red,

a dump truck,

 a plane,

and a sandy bear head.

I spy

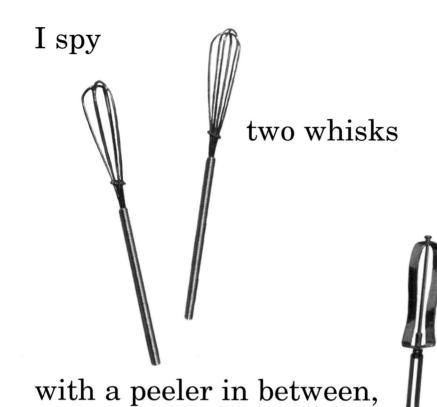

two whisks

with a peeler in between,

and three colored shakers:

yellow,

red,

green.

I spy

two fish,

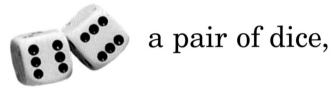 a pair of dice,

a golden shell,

 and a watermelon slice.

I spy

 a penny,

 a dragonfly,

 a horse-head coin,

 a pear,

 and MY.

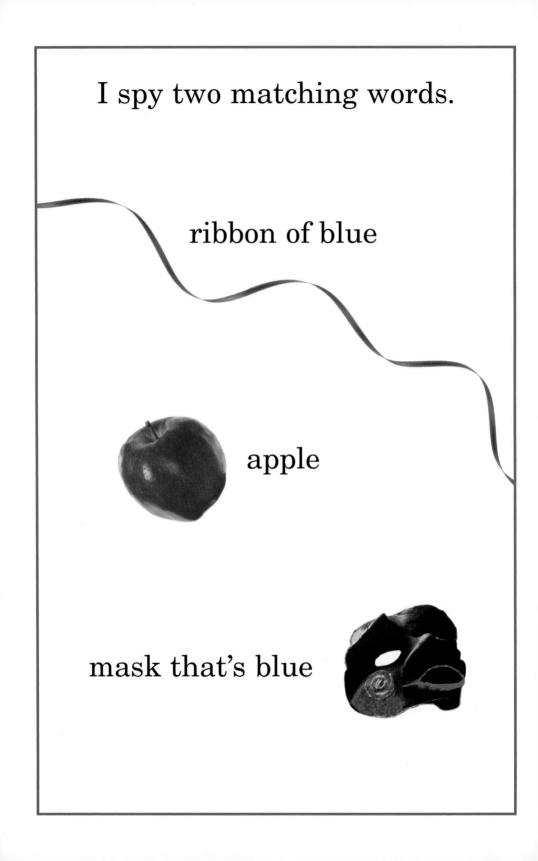

I spy two matching words.

ribbon of blue

apple

mask that's blue

# I spy two matching words.

two red caps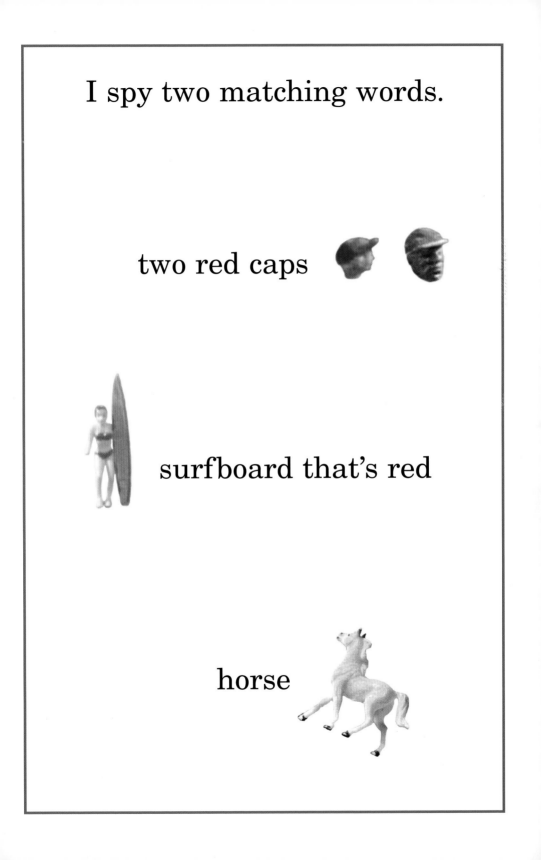

surfboard that's red

horse

I spy four words that
start with the letter B.

bunch of bananas

 penny

bunny that's brown

I spy two words that start with the letters SH.

 tomato

golden shell

three colored shakers

I spy three words that end with the letter R.

yellow car

 jar of glitter

bug that's blue

# I spy two words that end with the letters WN.

 orange

silly clown

 crown

# I spy two words that rhyme.

 ice cream cone

dump truck

 watermelon slice

# I spy two words that rhyme.

sailboat

pear

sandy bear head

# Collect the I Spy books

## Classics

# Collect the I Spy books

## Challengers

Also available are *I Spy A to Z*, *I Spy Spectacular*,
I Spy early readers, I Spy Little board books,
I Spy square paperbacks, and *I Spy Phonics Fun*.

Find all the I Spy books and more at
www.scholastic.com/ispy/.